OF ANGER AND OF GLEE

As the child grows up, he learns to moderate his expressions of anger and of glee, and he even learns to conceal his emotions.
—Robert Woodworth in "Psychology"

Of Anger and of Glee

By

SUZANNE E. GUETTEL

BOSTON
BRUCE HUMPHRIES, INC.
PUBLISHERS

Copyright, 1947, by Bruce Humphries, Inc.

Printed in the United States of America

This is dedicated to you, my dear. If you find parts of it too outspoken, or too obvious, remember that poetry is the hoyden of literature. Remember, too, the words of Kahlil Gibran, in *The Prophet*. He said: "You would know in words that which you have always known in thought."

CONTENTS

Of Anger and Of Glee	11
Go Back!	27
Lend-Lease	28
To a Hedonist	29
"Don't Cry, Little Girl!"	30
Pax	31
Sixth Sense	33
Ripples	35
Royal Absolutism	36
Love Clings	37
Deadandbury Tales	38
Storm	45
Foolish Race	46
"Donna E Mobile"	47
Syncretism	48
"What Fools These Mortals Be"	49
Chaotica	50
Apostrophe	51

OF ANGER AND OF GLEE

OF ANGER AND OF GLEE

PART I

We lived in glee at Happenstance.
It was a large and comely manse.
The weather and its windy ways
Laid pattern to our childhood days.
The house was roomy, full of light;
People fell in love with it on sight.
My brother, Ken, and I, and parents, loved it so.
We left it only when our conscience bade us go.
If we left, the magic aura of Happenstance
Went with us. No taunt or glance
Of the world, or life at large
Could touch those in Happenstance's charge.
Ken was wiser, older far than I,
Who mooned about, alone and shy.
He was a great lad, full of life and vigor.
His scope, imagination, was much bigger
Than the world in which he found himself,
Despite its slendor and its wealth.
Ken was caustic on occasion, full of pity
Other times. He had a dog which he named Kitty!
In accordance with the Yankee rule,
Kenneth went to public school;
Wrote on the walls, and popped his gum.
He played a lot, and studied some.

Much like Archie, his best friend,
Ken's mind took a literary trend.
He shone in drama and public speaking;
Was sterling in English, and went around tweaking
The sausage-cover curls
Of all the pretty girls.
There were sleigh-rides and hay-rides and such,
And camp every summer, which didn't mean much.
He began to write before he was ten.
(I was crowding on six along about then.)
His heroines all were dainty and small,
While Ken himself grew strong and tall.
With zeal and with zest a story he'd tell.
Each new theory or theme from his brain he'd expel
Like a cannon shot to lodge in the breast
Of every reader, but gave Ken no rest.
One day his heroine came to life.
He vowed to us all he'd take her to wife.
At the time he was only about fifteen,
And Julie the same, but she stayed on the scene.
When Ken went to college, he found that his forte
Was soon over-run by his studies and sport.
Football claimed the strength of his build.
In science and math he proved himself skilled.
His dreams about Julie went into recess.
Fate was in session, though her nickname was Bess.
She was Queen of the Day at "home-coming" game,
And in Ken's heart she seemed the same
As all the women he might never meet,
He knelt at her feet.

They spent hours at concerts and, finally, Ken
Bought a "vic" and some records.   They listened again.
Bess had rooms in a charming old spot
Where Ken went to study, but not a lot.
Chopin, Debussy became Eros' slaves.
Bess led our Kenny into the waves
Of love, no—passion, no—lust.
Ken's writing gave hard birth to dust.
I always thought of Ken in glory,
Dashing down the field, dashing off a story,
But there were times when he wondered, "What's it all about?"
He needed more than Bess, more than a victory shout.
I think Ken needed purpose; that's why he'd fret and yearn.
Would it be trite to say he had a lot to learn?
To Happenstance he came for each vacation.
I lived just to meet him at the station.
Perhaps he saw Julie once or twice.
She was "really pretty," or "awfully nice."
In 1942 Ken went to war;
Amid the agony and gore
He flew.   Europe was the nest
In which to lay the egg of death.
Twenty-one years of life had given Ken
A taste of what he hoped to find again:
Not a world in anger, but in glee.
At least that's what he wrote to me
From Nuremberg, the prison camp
Where all the day he had to starve and tramp
The icy ground.   He bore it well,

But suffered for his pals who fell
At every battle point.   He wrote to Bess:

   "My dear, when all this mess
   Is done, we'll find a place
   Where we can love, and propagate the race,
   Providing it's the peace that's here to stay.
   It seems an eon since I went away
   From you . . . your hair . . . your smile . . .your gentle hands.
   What am I doing in these foreign lands?"

The answer came, but not from Bess Carew.
She had other things to do.
The answer came from Julie, who wrote and said:

   "Dear Ken, you were missing.   I was dead.
   Then came the news that you were safe
   But prisoner.   Though you must chafe
   For freedom, have faith.   It will come.
   Did you get the chocolate bars?   I sent you some.
   Your sister asked me to Happenstance
   Sometime ago, while you were still in France.
   She's charming, Ken, and full of fun.
   She has more beaux than anyone.
   Remember how she used to be so quiet?
   The USO has made her life a riot.
   But what a lovely home!   When I came in the drive,
   The wind told me you were alive
   And would come back someday.
   That old house must always have its way."

There was no word from Bess, so
Ken told himself the letter's route was slow.

The days dragged on, until one night,
In May of 1945,—a flash of blinding light,
A roar of motors,—and the Russians came.
In many German towns it was the same.
"Adjustment" was the word they used, the chaplains meant:
"Things won't be the way they were before you went."
Oh, Happenstance was standing there, just as it used to be,
And Mom and Dad were waiting on the steps with me,
But somehow Ken had found a need, perhaps a lack,
In coming back.
That first day dragged and sucked at all of us,
Though I was quiet, next to Mother's fuss.
Ken ruffled up my hair; "It's good to see you, Sis.
I think I know just what it is I miss.
Life at Happenstance has lost its grace.
I'm afraid I'll have to leave the place."
He didn't go, but sat around a week or two,
Then had Mother invite Bess out too.
Bess came, arrayed in smiles and color.
Beside her, all of us seemed duller.
She waved away the fact she hadn't written
Ken, and curled up in the sun—a kitten.
No!—a cat! All sophisticate and style
Was Bess. Once in a while
I'd notice Kenneth frown as though
There was something here he wouldn't like to know.
They laughed a lot and played great jokes
Upon each other. Even so, the folks
Didn't think that Ken was happy,
And once when she'd been sitting on his lap, we

[15]

Heard her angry now, and loud.
Kenneth shut the door, too proud
To let us know so soon
He'd been reaching for the air, and not the moon.
We heard her scream, "You fool!
Marry you? Go back to school!
This has been a pleasant interlude.
Say my farewells. I'd only be rude."
Kenneth didn't like the world for ages,
But he returned to life by stages,
And began to scribble bitterly.
Some of the stuff he read to me
Had tinges of merit. The characters shone.
All Ken wished was to be alone.
His eyes were full of reproach and grief,
Empty of love, devoid of belief.
Our family laid the blame on Bess.
I'll admit she helped it, yes;
But have you ever bombed a town;
Sat way up there and stared right down
At life which you annihilate at will?
Ken was never meant to kill;
Nor were a million, million other men,
All as fine and brave as Ken.
Julie came to call one afternoon.
I was afraid that she had come too soon
To fully blot out Bess, and languor,
To conquer Kenneth's deep-set anger.
I was wrong, for Julie Ross
Had gained wisdom with the cross

She bore through Ken's infatuation.
She roused him to his old elation
For the little things, like golf and swimming.
Every day was full and brimming
Over with a carefree zest.
Mother admitted, "Julie knows him best."
He saw his work in a different light.
His plots were real, and his characters right.
The message he wrote wasn't heavy or coarse,
And gone was the anger, gone the remorse.
He could rebuild what the war had upset.
He wasn't trapped in the flail, in the net.
The fourteenth of August brought surcease from strife
To the world, and to Kenneth—a wife.

PART II

The very poor end of our city was called
River Row.   There lived Archibald.
Archie was born in a dark little room,
And all of his childhood was laden with gloom.
It hurt to leave Happenstance for the River,
But it was Arch, not I, who was the giver
In our friendship, which began
With the public school's alphabetical plan.
For Archie's name was Eaton, and I am Kenneth Elby.
The lack of love in Archie's home might well be
What first drew us together,
For we weren't birds of a feather.
Archie's principal quirk
Was a disinclination to work.
It's not that he was very lazy,
But he was just a little hazy
About the sort of thing he liked to do,
Until music came along, and then he knew.
Where music reigned, discretion did not enter in.
Archie wore our operatic records thin,
But also gloried in Bing's latest platter,
And any listening ear he'd shatter
With a patriotic Sousa march
Or some Goodman jazz, that Arch.

His manners were not good, but I noticed he was able
To eat quite nicely, when invited to our table.
Though he was used to shabby places, and to swearing men,
He'd say, "I like your house, your family, Ken."
But he never showed by wistful word or glance
That he wished he'd come from Happenstance.
We both hit high school with a thud.
Compared to Arch's popularity, I was a dud.
He had a dance-band with a fancy name,
THE FALLEN ARCHES, and my Dad thought it a shame
That a guy with so much talent should
Throw it away for good
On swing. But Arch gave me one reason,
"The dough from this will keep the folks from freezin'."
The heart and hearth of River Row
Was hardly warm enough for snow.
Archie grew up somewhat faster than I.
Have you noticed how comfort gives Time the lie?
Archie had need of some other assurance
That life was more than just plain endurance,
While I knew all that I needed to know
Right in the prelude to the Big Show.
He left me quite breathless one Saturday night
By saying he'd see me on Sunday all right,
But now Mabel was standing down the street.
He didn't want to keep her too long on her feet.
I teased and I taunted, called Mabel his girl,
Said she was ugly, had eyes like a squirrel.
But Archie was blunter than usual with me.
He was tired of youngsters, and I was one, you see.

"Naw, Mabel's the one I sleep with, Ken!
My girl, the real one, is Dorothy Wren!"
I let out my breath in a slow sort of gasp.
My hand was quite limp in Archibald's clasp.
Sunday came and we went fishing.
The whole day long I couldn't help wishing
That last night's talk would disappear.
I was full of curiosity and fear.
Apparently Arch thought no more of it,
He stared at the willow, the sky above it,
And suddenly whistled a few bars of song.
He worked at the melody all day long.
By nightfall he'd written the words and the tune
To a song—all willow trees and June.
I think I caught the difference then
Of how he felt about Dorothy Wren.
Dottie's family and mine were friends,
So she and Arch lived at opposite ends
Of the town, and the so-called social level.
Society was my friend's very private devil.
Dorothy beamed when Archie played for dances,
Or walked with her through Happenstance's
Lovely grounds, but she often let him know
She couldn't be seen near River Row.
Mabel on the other hand, while not so pure,
Informed Archie many times that she was sure
His very roots in River Row would be
As great a benefit to him as mine would be to me.
As I gained years and wisdom, so did I gain respect
For Mabel. With all her love for Arch she did affect

No airs, no pretense, though she might have done so.
She had met Dot. She seemed to realize, to know
That Archie sought a way of life
That Dot might give him, as his wife.
I wonder if she saw by then
How shallow and how false the Wren
Was turning out to be. Poor Archibald!
My sister said Dot was a fool, and called
Her every name she'd ever heard.
Sis revelled in the printed word
Her brother wrote just then, and knew
Some horrid names. There were even a few
Beyond Miss Elby's knowledge.
When I went off to Philadelphia and college,
Arch came along. He took a welder's job by day
And played in bands at night. That way
He sent money home, and still he had enough
To keep him going. He led a rough
And rowdy life, until he got a break.
One night over onions and steak
He told me of the music, "Lucky Seven."
You'd thought he'd found the road to Heaven.
He'd sold a musical, score and all,
To a Broadway show, opening in the fall
Of 1942. He thought he'd touched success,
And Archie really had, I guess.
We never saw the opening, because by then
We were learning to live like fighting men.
We were down in Texas, learning to fly.
We were going to war, Archibald and I.

Bess came down to camp for a visit one week
And after she left, Archie saw fit to speak
To me in sterner tones than ever before.
He said, "Ken, don't see her any more.
She's not your sort, but Julie is."
I got sore, asked him what business it was of his.
I pointed out that he and Dot were worlds apart,
And yet he tried to keep her in his heart.
He gave me the old answer, "With us it's different, Ken."
It was weeks before we could be friends again.
We got our wings. Arch was my bombardier.
The time for going across was drawing near.
Arch went home on leave to see his Dot,
And though I went home, too, I was with Bess a lot.
The day before we left for France
Arch came out to Happenstance.
We roamed the place with Sis.
He said, "This is one spot I'll really miss.
Now's the time to tell you, Ken . . .
When we get back . . . Dot and I'll be married then."
Congratulations were in order, and of course,
Arch and I got drunk. We sang ourselves hoarse
And fell into bed for a last night's sleep
At home. He asked me to keep
The engagement a secret because
That was the Wren's special war-clause.
One day over there we decided to name the plane.
We had the whole day to do it, thanks to some rain.
Arch was the favorite of the whole crew
And so we said, "The name is up to you."

He called her Mighty Mabel,
And when we left the table
He took me aside and said he'd thought better
Of naming her Dot. He'd had no letter
From Dottie in days.
He said those were Dottie's ways.
After a particularly hellish mission
Arch and I both got permission
To take three-day leave across the channel.
Whoever said that life's not banal?
When we got back Arch had a letter
Waiting from Dot, but thought better
Of opening it until we got back
From a flight that sent us into the flak
Of a bunch of Nazis who brought us down,
After we rained hell on a German town.
Arch saved my life, and another guy's too.
I told him, "That medal will look good on you!"
His leg was shot up, and couldn't walk,
But while we lay there he started to talk.
He patched us up and did what he could
To make us forget the pain and the blood.
How he stood it himself I'll never know.
He thought only of me, and the gunner, Joe.
They finally found us, the Germans, the Huns.
They told us to walk, pushed us with their guns.
Joe and I must have passed out cold;
Archie tried to do as he was told.
We reached Nuremberg, all three on one litter,
Numb with our pain, and angry, not bitter.

Weeks later the mail began to arrive.
I'm sure it's what kept us alert and alive.
Arch's leg kept on hurting, but didn't seem worse.
His letters from home were illiterate, terse.
He kept on watching for that one letter
From Dot, which he had thought better
Of opening back in France.
Meanwhile I read him news from Happenstance.
He fell into coma one April day.
For one whole week like that he lay.
They did what they could, gave him medical care.
The letter caught up with us while he lay there.
He awoke one morning and smiled at the guys.
He asked for his letter, but some blessed and wise
Hand made me open it first, thank the Lord.
I read it, re-read it, held tight to the board
Of his cot and said loud,
"Wait until I get rid of this crowd."
The fellows filed out so I could suggest
That if I read it to him, he could go on and rest.
He tired quickly and agreed with the plan.
I've never felt such outraged pity for another man.
I had the letter in my hand, but words came from my head
As I turned and faced Archie, dying on his bed.
"I'll read it to you in a minute; be right back."
I was good and sick outside that shack.
They handed me some more of Archie's mail,
And though I felt my conscience and my courage fail,
I opened a letter from Mabel.
As soon as I was able

I took both letters in to Arch, who said,
"If you hadn't come, I'd have gotten out of bed.
Read me that letter from Dot, and read it now.
I'm not sure I'll be around to hear it later, somehow."
I sat down to read, with a word both comforting and gay:

   "My Arch, forgive delay.
   But all the things I want to say
   Sound foolish when I write.
   I dream of you each night,
   And before dreaming, pray
   That we will know one day
   Such love as all the poets write about.
   And when we've grown gray and stout
   We'll still love one another so!
   You're anxious about your musical, I know.
   It's a huge success, as I expected
   They think it's going to be elected
   To run another year, and then
   You'll be able to see it once again!
   Its music charms all those who hear it.
   And do you know that being near it
   Makes me feel closer to you?
   It keeps me from being quite so blue.
   Be happy, Arch, if you are able."

And of course the letter was signed, "Mabel,"
But I substituted Dot, and lied.
I'm glad I did, for Archie died
Not long after that. Before he died he said.
"Ken, I knew as sure as that I'm on this bed,
My Dot would feel the way I do
About our future, and we'll have one, too!

That letter sounds just like her, bless her heart."
I thought that I might fall apart
Just standing by his bed. Somehow
It seems a little thing I did there now.
Dorothy's letter, as you must have guessed,
Though written half in earnest, half in jest,
Informed a hero named Archibald Eaton
That he had been quite badly beaten
On his homeground, by some gent
Who changed Dot's name from Wren to Brent!
I suppose one person's life
Can't be compared to all the world in strife,
But Arch, my friend, is dead. He fought.
And, I ask myself, has all that been for naught?
We're looking for a world, guys like Arch and me:
Not a world of anger, but of glee.

GO BACK!

You don't change your mind about life in a day.
I wonder why Fate doesn't work it that way.
How simple you'd find it
(And how little you'd mind it!)
If all the trite phrases were true.
("Out of sight, out of mind"; "we're through.")
Your memory is treasonably bright.
The wilder the weather, the further the flight.
You haven't a chance of escaping from thought.
Go back! Go back before you're caught!
You haven't a chance to bargain with Fate.
No, I'm afraid it's much too late.
But just in case Fate lends you an ear,
Remember whom you're forgetting, my dear.

LEND-LEASE

My blood, my thought, my heart God gave
To one who must be very brave.
God took my blood from out my vein
And said, "It can no longer stain."
God took my thought from out my mind
And said, "From now your brain is blind."
God took my heart from out my chest
And said, "No more will you have rest."
My blood, my thought, my heart God gave
To one I know is very brave.

TO A HEDONIST

Tread hard upon the toes of worry.
From tears and sadness onward scurry.
Neglect the sick of heart and mind.
Flock closely next those of your kind.
Study only games and jesting.
Venture not outside your nesting.
For your world would fast decay.
Onward! Unexpected rainy day!

Stay on in dreamy climes of pleasure.
Think all of life is fun and leisure.
Meet up with sorrow as a foe.
The way of the unheeding go.
Forget the evil after men.
At life you'll laugh; remember then
That others suffer in your stead;
That others for your wounds have bled.

"DON'T CRY, LITTLE GIRL!"

"Don't cry, little girl!"
They said to me
When I fell and hurt my arm;
And they were right to speak to me
For it really did no harm.

"Don't cry, little girl!"
They cautioned me
When I bumped and bruised my head;
And they were right to caution me
For I only hurt the bed.

"Don't cry, little girl!"
They scolded me
When I scratched a "skeeter" bite;
And once again, I must agree,
The grown-ups were right.

"Don't cry, little girl!"
Once more they said
When I fell and broke my heart,
But the little girl and I were very far apart!

PAX

Down through the darkness came a ray of light;
The world was sane again, and right.
Missouri mules were sleeping in the sun.
The Kansas farmer threw away his gun.
In Wisconsin the people cheered, and then
They called across the lake to Michigan.
The Iowans once more plowed their corn,
While Georgians blew loud on Victory's horn.
The Dakotas and Carolinas, too,
All watched the grey, o'er burdened sky turn blue.
Louisiana turned its back on war.
Kentucky danced down Freedom's corridor.
Staid Massachusetts sang loud the hymn
With Maine and Vermont, for it was no whim
That Rhode Island, New Hampshire, New York,
And New Jersey could come out of their ark
Into a dry world where Connecticut
And fellow-states were not the butt
Of some madman's aim to conquer our world.
O'er Maryland and Delaware unfurled
The flag that bore us through the loathsome days
Where Alabama's, Florida's highways
Were filled with men who were but going to die.
Hear Pennsylvania and Ohio cry,
"We have won the battle and deserve a rest!"
The Virginias and Mississippi could attest
That they all aided in the efforts too.
Then Texas and Nevada yelled, "Yahoo!"

Yes, Tennessee, Utah, and Illinois
All wept with other states in greatest joy.
The Minnesotans and Nebraska's men
Were all through playing the tragedian.
The oil in Oklahoma spouted high
As if Arkansas to notify
That Victory and Peace were ours in truth.
From Indiana, Idaho, the youth
And aged too began a song and dance,
While Montana and Washington in the gloaming
Joined the chorus, along with Wyoming.
Then Oregon and California bowed
While Colorado and New Mexico vowed
That never again would we live in fear
Of the foe who held false tyranny dear.
The state of Arizona quick agreed
To e'er uphold the democratic creed.
The last proud voice which cried throughout the land
Was Washington, D. C., our wonderland.
I was afraid I'd awake, afraid I'd find
That sleep had played tricks with a pliant mind.
But mistake it not for delirium.
All I have written has actually come!

(August, 1945)

SIXTH SENSE

Man says Man has only five
Senses on which he does thrive.
But I maintain that Man's not right,
For God has made, of His own might,
A sixth sense.

God gave us eyes with which to see,
But does Man really think that He
Gave us two eyes only for
External beauty, nothing more ...
A sixth sense?

God gave us ears with which to hear,
But does Man think that with the ear
Only sounds of earth are heard,
Or else a kind of unspoken word ...
A sixth sense?

God gave us sense with which to smell,
But is it just a flowerbell
That Man must scent,
Or is there sweeter meant
A sixth sense?

God gave us, too, a sense of taste.
Does Man need this but to waste
Upon food we find at table,
Or of more are we able ...
A sixth sense?

God gave us sense with which to feel,
But does Man only count as real
His very touch, or does he hope,
Underneath Life's twisted rope,
For a sixth sense?

I maintain that Man's not right.
I maintain that God's own might,
The might, the truth above,
Has fashioned love . . .
The sixth sense.

RIPPLES

I feel like a great discoverer.
I just found out today
That though you love forever,
Your love's reborn each day!

Anti-climax is my name.
People point to me with shame.
And yet, I can't help walking in
On the crest of every sin!

No clock that tells the time of day
Could measure it in any way.
No mark upon it could I set;
Nor yet upon it any debt—
Being with you!

My hopes? My aims? They're not so high.
Perhaps that's why
Though I carried them,
Someone else married them!

ROYAL ABSOLUTISM

In the midst of a democratic nation
I seem to still retain the station
Of obedient subject to a king.
Monarchy's a hectic thing.
His majesty is unconcerned
With all but the homage he has earned.
I bow and scrape for all I'm worth,
Only to face his mocking and mirth.
His every word is my command,
But I dare not touch his hand.
I am a lowly vassal at his feet;
With humility his glance I meet.
Though he be Lord and I be slave,

Though I be coward and he be brave,
The monarchy I'd not give up.
The monarch must his ego sup.
I can't hear that freedom ring!
Health to the monarch! God save the king!

LOVE CLINGS

It's well that you should leave me here and just forget;
But are you sure that you've forgotten yet?...
A kiss, a glance, a ride along the Bay?...
My dear, you were so earnest in your play.
Though you are occupied with other things,
Have you brushed off the lint of love?
It clings.

DEADANDBURY TALES

(With the usual apologies to the unusual Chaucer!)

It was about September Third
When I received important word
That I must go to Washington,
And so my journey was begun.
The last night out I parked my car
At an hotel, the Alcazar.
'Twas there I met the twenty folk
Whose LEADER shook my hand and spoke;
"My friend, you see us gathered here
About to heave the poisoned spear.
For we are going to Washington.
We must complain, yes, everyone!"
The speaker was a pallid man
Who needed more than just a tan.
His eyes were sunken in and vague;
He breathed as though he had the ague.
He wore a shirt of dirty grey,
And pants that knew a better day.
"Of what do you complain?" I asked.
"Well, friend," he said, "my fam'ly basked
In health and happiness until
The sewer ran into our rooms
And gagged us all with its foul fumes.
The Cap'talists are all to blame.
The senators should hide in shame."
I gathered that this orator
Would enter in the Senate door.

He'd make a speech so he'd be sure
That Congress would rebuild his sewer!
Next to him stood a real OLD MAID.
She was both flat-chested and staid.
"Look here, young man," she pointed out,
"I know what life is all about!
I cannot rest until they've passed
A bill to have all harlots gassed.
Why, no man's safe along the street,
Though what I say is not discreet."
A frustrate maid on Cap'tal Hill
Could hardly introduce a bill!
Mind you, a war has just been fought,
But all the pilgrims, they cared naught
That government must concentrate
To safely guide the bark of state
Between the rocks and bars of sand,
In fervent search of Peaceful Land!
A TEACHER spoke from out the crowd,
"Dear Sir, if I may be allowed
To tell you of my innovation,
I know a way to stop inflation.
Let each man sign up for my course
And he shall live without remorse!"
In other words this rotund owl
Would try to agitate and howl
'Till all the politicians knew
That teachers can make errors, too!
Then came a MOTHER with FOUR GIRLS
(All of whom wore rib-length curls!)

She thought a poster they would make,
Entitled "Fight, for children's sake!"
She said that they were lovely girls,
But, oh my God, those rib-length curls!
The only poster they'd inspire:
USE THESE POSTERS FOR A FIRE!
A learned DOCTOR rose to speak.
At that I watched with tongue in cheek.
"If all the world could just get sick,
I'd make this peace.   I'm very quick."
The doctor's foolish recipe
Would hardly cook up Victory.
A voice arose as from a well:
"I speak to you, agent of Hell.
The Devil hates Democracy
And so he has appointed me
His ORACLE throughout the land.
The Congress must give me a hand."
Believe me, he was of this earth,
For he had height, and quite a girth.
And yet there seemed about his face
Unhealthy glow, and little grace.
His helpmate was exotic, young,
But seemed to lack a voice and tongue.
This WAITRESS charmed us with her smile,
But held us back yet all the while.
These people really were like you.
They had homes and families, too.
They knew about love, of passion,
And yet they found the fashion

Of plaint to Senate and to House
Of greater meaning and pretense,
Than all the peace and its defense.
A DRUGGIST then came to the front.
"My friends," he said, "may I be blunt?
I pull the wings off helpless flies,
So I'm suspected by Martin Dies!"
The shouts of laughter and of glee
Made it impossible to see
The druggist's face, so I could tell
If he were kidding, or not well.
I gathered that he was about
To put our old Martin right out!
A MOVIE STAR was next to talk.
She said, "You know, they've made me walk!
They say I can't have gasoline
To fill my big black limousine!"
She wore her hair over one eye
And that may be the reason why
But half of life she really knew.
(I think I know which half. Do you?)
A LAWYER came before the group
(Which looked more like a circus troop!)
And there began a detailed brief.
The man looked much like fatted beef.
His face was red; his neck was thick,
And nothing but his pulse was quick.
"Kind gentlemen," he started out,
"The Supreme Court without a doubt
Needs some new blood and some new brain."
At this point I boarded a train

[41]

Of thought that led me far astray.
I could not help but contemplate
The pints of blood he could donate
To Red Cross banks throughout the land,
And yet that crowd gave him a hand!
They listened to this popinjay,
Admiring his false roundelay.
A long-haired, long-eared old baboon
Arose to chant his foolish tune.
"I write the history of man,
For I am an HISTORIAN.
How could I write about this war
When every man in every corps
Received me with a censor near?"
Enough of that old chanticleer!
The next loud voice was that of Art.
A PAINTER rose to take his part.
"I paint the portraits very well,
But none of this war bagatelle
Shall spoil my genius or my style.
I'll paint out every Anglophile!
I'll scrape off every Russian face!
Why should we salvage their disgrace?
That's Hitler's job, and not for us.
Excuse me while I paint a bus!"
So he would not help our Allies . . . ,
A "paper-hanger" in disguise!
A SOCIALITE was next in line.
"My dear, the food here is divine!
But when those fools in Washingtton
Start rationing my venison

I fear New York will then deter
Me from the Social Register!"
A DEBUTANTE she had for child,
Who looked at me and when she smiled
I thought, "Here is a girl who's real."
And then she made my blood congeal
By screeching out "I'll teach that bum
That her daughter is not so dumb.
If I can't have that new mink fur
I'll tell on her and the chauffeur!"
By this time I was really ill,
And knew that I had drunk my fill
Of these vile pilgrims who were bound
Their foolish theories to expound
In Washington to those great men
Who worked for every citizen.
There was another man to hear,
And so I lent a tired ear,
"The Country's thirsty for its Scotch,
An' I would even bet that lotch
Of you good men think I am drrrrunk!
Well, lemme tell you that is bunk!
I only had a fifth at home,
Jusssss so I could really show'm
How happy men can be with Scotch.
Say! What are all them pinkish spotch?"
THE DRUNKARD fell flat on his face.
I was prepared to leave the place.
But first I had a job to do.
"Do you know me? Well, I know you.

I've been to fight so you'll stay free,
What have you been doing for me?"
A SOLDIER in a khaki coat,
A guy just old enough to vote
Was I, and not too good with words,
But I knew what to tell those birds.
"Sure, your Senators make mistakes!
Of course the House has sev'ral fakes!
But we're the ones who put them there!
From President down to Mayor,
The people vote as they see fit,
And say! that's not the half of it!
Impeach the men who do you dirt!
Don't be afraid! You won't get hurt!
Don't tear down all the things you've built!
Don't cry over what's spoilt or spilt!
Thank God you're free, and had a chance
To stamp out all intolerance.
What? You're going home, you're leaving here?
Well, what the Hell! . . . buy me a beer!"

And so the weary Pilgrims' star
Had led them to the Alcazar,
But if they go to Washington,
They won't complain; no, nary one!

STORM

The sun rose with her rising fears.
The clouds sailed around like flying spears.
The rain began to fall, a pattern for her tears.
The thunder called out, loud, ironic cheers.

She drifted aimlessly about until
The lightning spied her at the window-sill.
The rain stopped. The earth had drunk its fill.
Her fear ran on, as in a grinding-mill.

Though well she knew the struggle was for naught,
She struggled to cast off all thought.
Surcease from storm to Nature God had brought,
But ever storm to Mankind He has taught.

FOOLISH RACE

She kept each mem'ry polished bright.
She called each meeting to her sight.
She made each moment live again.
She, of the foolish race of men . . .

She remembered every word and whim,
Just as she knew the look of him.
She wrote all down and read it then.
She, of the foolish race of men . . .

She'd only mem'ry of him left.
At preying she had not been deft.
She was no eagle, but a wren.
She, of the foolish, foolish race of men . . .

"DONNA E MOBILE"

The sweetest wine is sour;
The whitest cloud is black;
The darkness stops beyond the dawn,
When I am not with Jack.

The fire dies at kindle;
The brightest sun is wan;
The water turns to icicles,
When I am not with Don.

The coal-fuel turns to dust;
The lean meat turns to fat;
The clock goes round from right to left,
When I am not with Pat.

'Tis only when she's out a lot,
Mid admirers and bouquets;
'Tis only when she's flattered much,
That nights will follow days.

SYNCRETISM

The moon's not far away tonight
Compared to you.   You're out of sight.
A voice says, "No! He loves me not!"
Another pleads, "He cares a lot."
A third one wails, "How can I know?"
And all declare, "I love him so!"

The moon grows weary of my tale.
He thinks I speak to no avail.
He yawns and says, "Now go to bed."
He sadly shakes his silver head.
The street-lights flirt with that bright moon,
But they shall find out all too soon
That they are but a crumb of light
To that great sphere's bold appetite.

You, too, are great! Then, pray, am I
But a faint glimmer in your sky?
Rather than worship from afar,
Let me at least become a star.

"WHAT FOOLS THESE MORTALS BE"

"What fools these mortals be"
That they simply can't see
How tender is feeling;
How long takes the healing.

"What fools these mortals be"
To make one pay the fee
Of broken heart all crushed
When solace is hushed.

"What fools these mortals be"
Who do not heed a plea
For love and trust from friends,
But take to haughty trends.

"What fools these mortals be,"
And why are you pointing at me?

CHAOTICA

I fell into Chaos the other day,
Because on earth I'd lost my way.
I hadn't sinned; ah! that I knew;
So what did I there, in that *rendezvous*?
A lonely feeling that rose in my throat
Gave vent to a memory quite remote.
On earth I had been lonely.

I searched all through Chaos to find a friend,
When suddenly down at the very end
In gloomy surroundings I saw
A kindred soul, and stood in awe.
He too had fallen from the land.
We found our way back, hand in hand.
On earth he had been lonely.

APOSTROPHE

A plane flew overhead,
And so I played instead
Of sitting sanely here below
We were up there in flight. I know,
You've often said I do pretend
These silly dreams for Time on end,
But if you'd seen the sky
You would not need to ask me why.

A car sped by so fast!
Yet hardly had it passed
But we were in it, you and I,
And we were passing others by.
You laugh at me, but could you know
What sights we saw! where we did go!
You'd laugh with joy to think
I took you so near Heaven's brink.

We passed a field of blue,
And passing, still I stopped with you
In my own mind. The flowers bent
In reverence to dreams that sent
Me there with you. (And still you smile?)
Had you but seen the wooden stile
That leads to other fields,
You'd like what my "imagine" yields.

We passed a house with children there.
Though you drove on, we climbed the stair.
The children welcomed us. We stayed
With them, and there I truly played
As though our life had found its dream.
How sad that it may only "seem."

For foolish as this all may "seem,"
It is to me more than a dream.
It's wish, and prayer, and hope, and plea . . .
A broken heart's apostrophe.